THRESHER SHARKS

THE SHARK DISCOVERY LIBRARY

Sarah Palmer

Illustrated by Ernest Nicol and Libby Turner

Rourke Enterprises, Inc.
Vero Beach, Florida 32964

© 1988 Rourke Enterprises, Inc.

Library of Congress Cataloging-in-Publication Data

Palmer, Sarah, 1955-
   Thresher Sharks/Sarah Palmer; illustrated by Ernest
Nicol and Libby Turner

      p. cm. — (The Sharks discovery library)
   Includes index.
   Summary: Describes the appearance, habitat, and
behavior of thresher sharks.
   ISBN 0-86592-460-0
   1. Alopiidae — Juvenile literature. 2. Sharks-
Juvenile literature.   [1. Thresher sharks. 2. Sharks]
I. Nicol, Ernest ill.   II. Title.
III. Series: Palmer,Sarah,1955-
Sharks discovery library.
QL638.95.A4P35   1989   88-6428
597'.31 - dc19   CIP
                               AC

TABLE OF CONTENTS

THRESHER SHARKS

Thresher sharks take their name from their long tail fins, which lash through the water. The upper part, or **lobe**, of the tail fin is longer than that of any other shark. It sometimes grows to be as long as the body of the shark itself. These tails make thresher sharks some of the easiest sharks to recognize.

resher sharks have very long tail fins

HOW THEY LOOK

The largest thresher shark known was over 18 feet long. Its weight was probably about half a ton. An average-sized male thresher is about 11 feet long. The females are slightly larger, usually about 15 feet long. Thresher sharks have stout bodies, which are dark blue-gray on their backs and white underneath. Sometimes their skin is slightly mottled. The most noticeable thing about a thresher shark is its long tail fin.

Male and female thresher shark

WHERE THEY LIVE

Thresher sharks like to live in warm waters. They are often seen in the oceans off Florida and Southern California. Thresher sharks usually stay in deep water and do not come close to shore. Two smaller **species** of thresher sharks, the Smalltooth Thresher and the Bigeye Thresher, are sometimes found in shallower seas.

Thresher sharks usually live in deep water

WHAT THEY EAT

Thresher sharks live on fish. Their diet includes mackerel, herring, shad, and pilchard—each a different kind of fish. Thresher sharks hunt in groups. They follow schools of fish, herding them together with their long tails. Scientists believe that thresher sharks hit and stun the fish with their tail fins to make them easier to catch. Sometimes by mistake they hit birds that skim the surface of the ocean.

Thresher sharks herd a school of fish with their tails

Thresher sharks like warm waters

Thresher sharks' tail fins
should be avoided!

THEIR JAWS AND TEETH

Thresher sharks have small, triangular teeth. They are not very dangerous. All sharks have five or more sets of teeth in their mouth, but only one set that you can see. The rest are folded down inside their mouths. When a shark loses or breaks a tooth, another one grows up to replace it. A shark may go through a hundred sets of teeth in its lifetime.

Thresher sharks have small triangular teeth

BABY THRESHER SHARKS

Female thresher sharks give birth to live young. They swim to a place they know to be safe for the babies while they are small. The water must be warm and have enough food for the young sharks. The mother shark must be careful, because the baby sharks will have to look after themselves from the moment they are born. Each year a female thresher will bear two to four babies. At birth the babies are 4 or 5 feet long.

Baby thresher sharks take car of themselves as soon as the are born

SHARK ATTACK!

Not all sharks are dangerous. Thresher sharks are one of the harmless species of sharks. There are no known cases where threshers have attacked humans. Probably the most dangerous part of a thresher shark is its strong tail fin. If you were hit by that, it would be like being whipped with something very sharp.

Thresher sharks are not dangerous

THEIR SENSES

Most sharks do not have very good hearing. Their ears are more important for balance and finding direction. An extra sense called the **lateralis system** helps sharks find **prey** on which to feed. As well as hearing the movement of fish close by, sharks can feel their **vibrations** through their lateralis systems. This means that they can attack their prey faster.

Thresher sharks use their lateralis system to find food

FACT FILE

Common Name: Thresher Shark
Scientific Name: Aliopas vulpinas
Color: Dark blue-gray
Average Size: Male   – 11 feet, 9 inches
     Female – 15 feet, 1 inch
Where They Live: Warm waters, offshore
Danger Level: No danger

Glossary

lateralis system (lat er AL is SYS tem) — a sense which helps sharks find objects by feeling their movements

lobe (LOBE) — the fleshy part of a shark's tail fin

prey (PREY) — an animal that is hunted for food

species (SPE cies) — a scientific term meaning kind or type

vibrations (vi BRA tions) — sounds or movements that can be felt

INDEX